The Art of Black Silent Book with Happy End War Story From Ukraine
2016

BY ADAM HUDAIB   adamhudaib@gmail.com

I0478803

In this unique book with a special silent design
There is No words to Read ....
Just go throw the pages and the Pictures will
Evoke your Emotions
In the next edition I will submit the full story
in words..
For Original Materials Please Contact me...

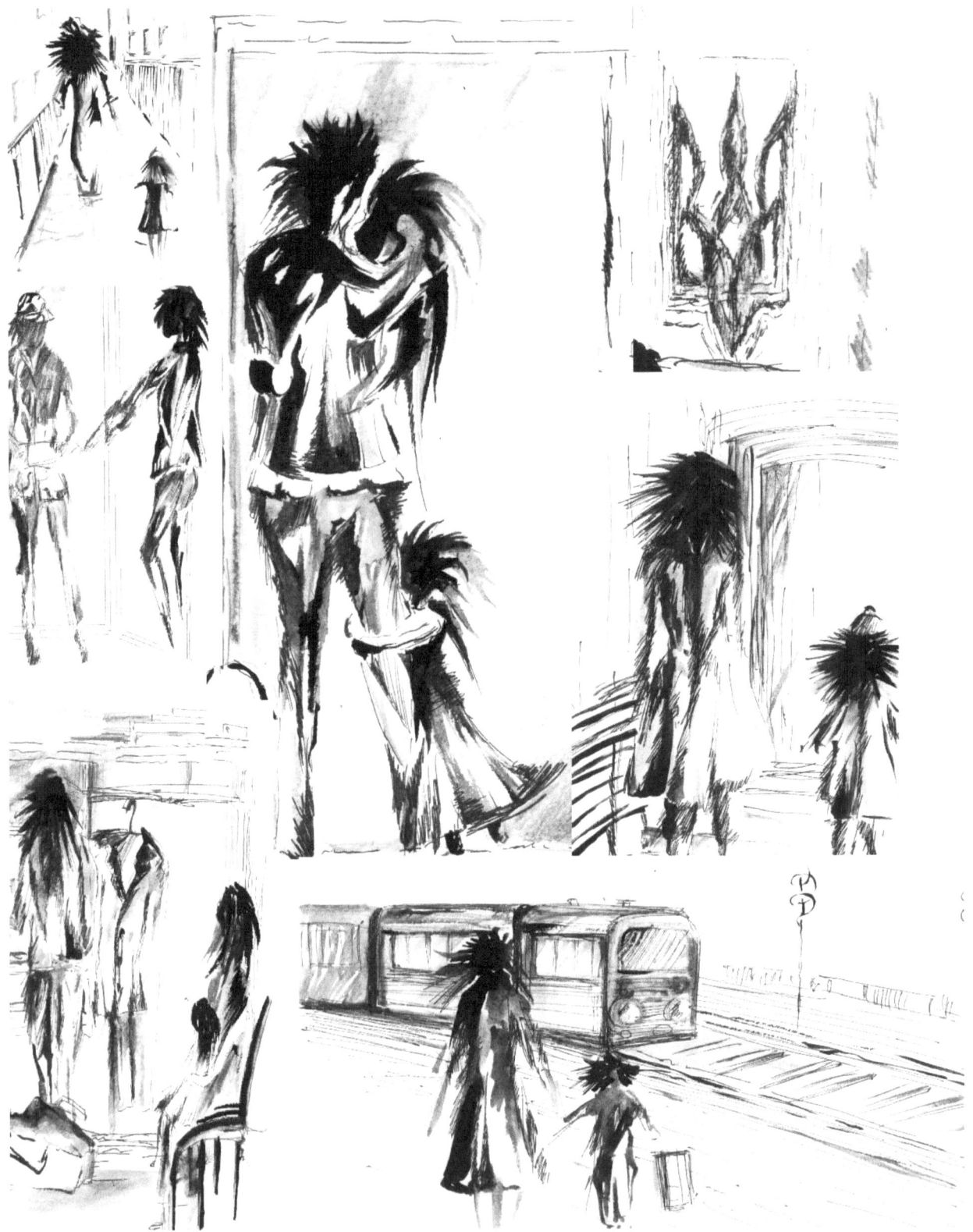

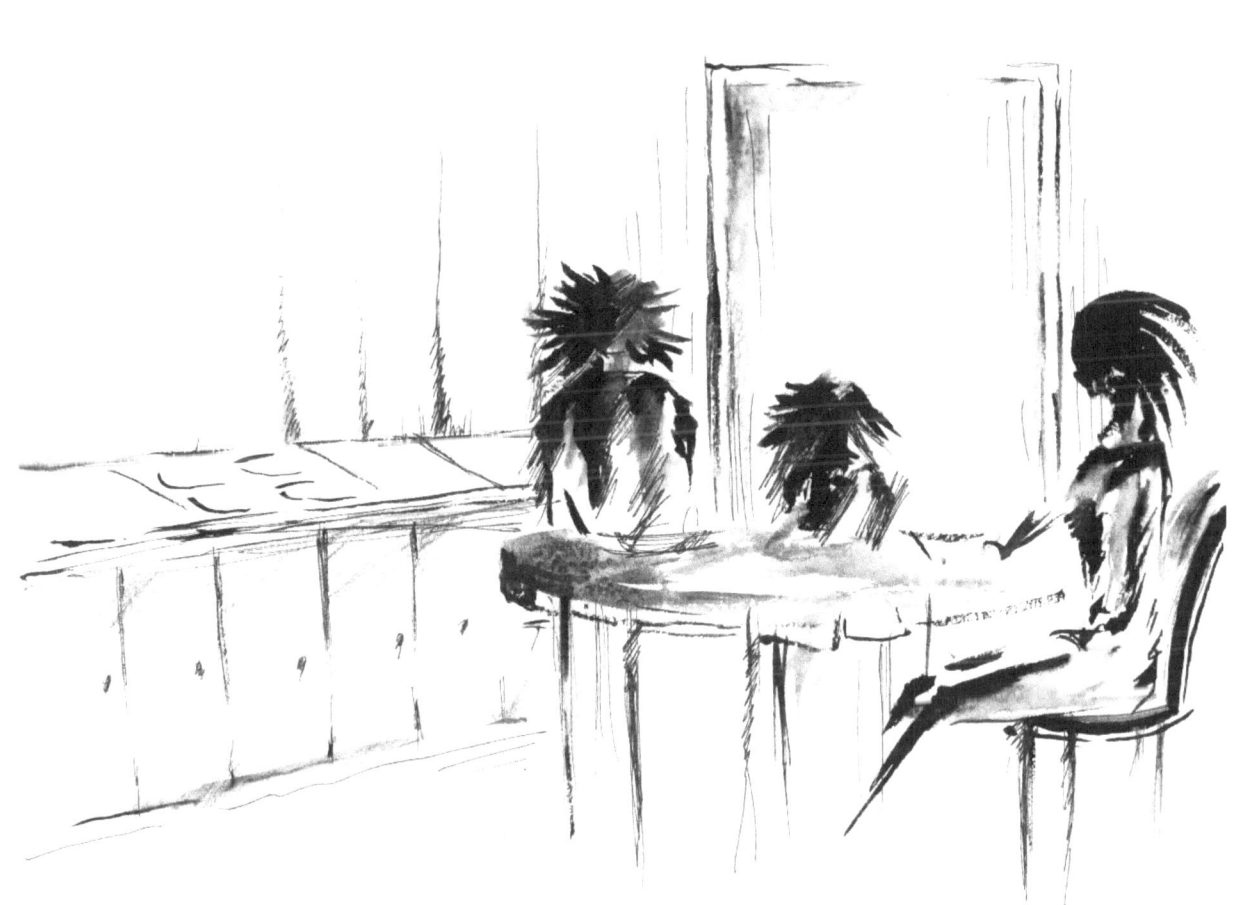

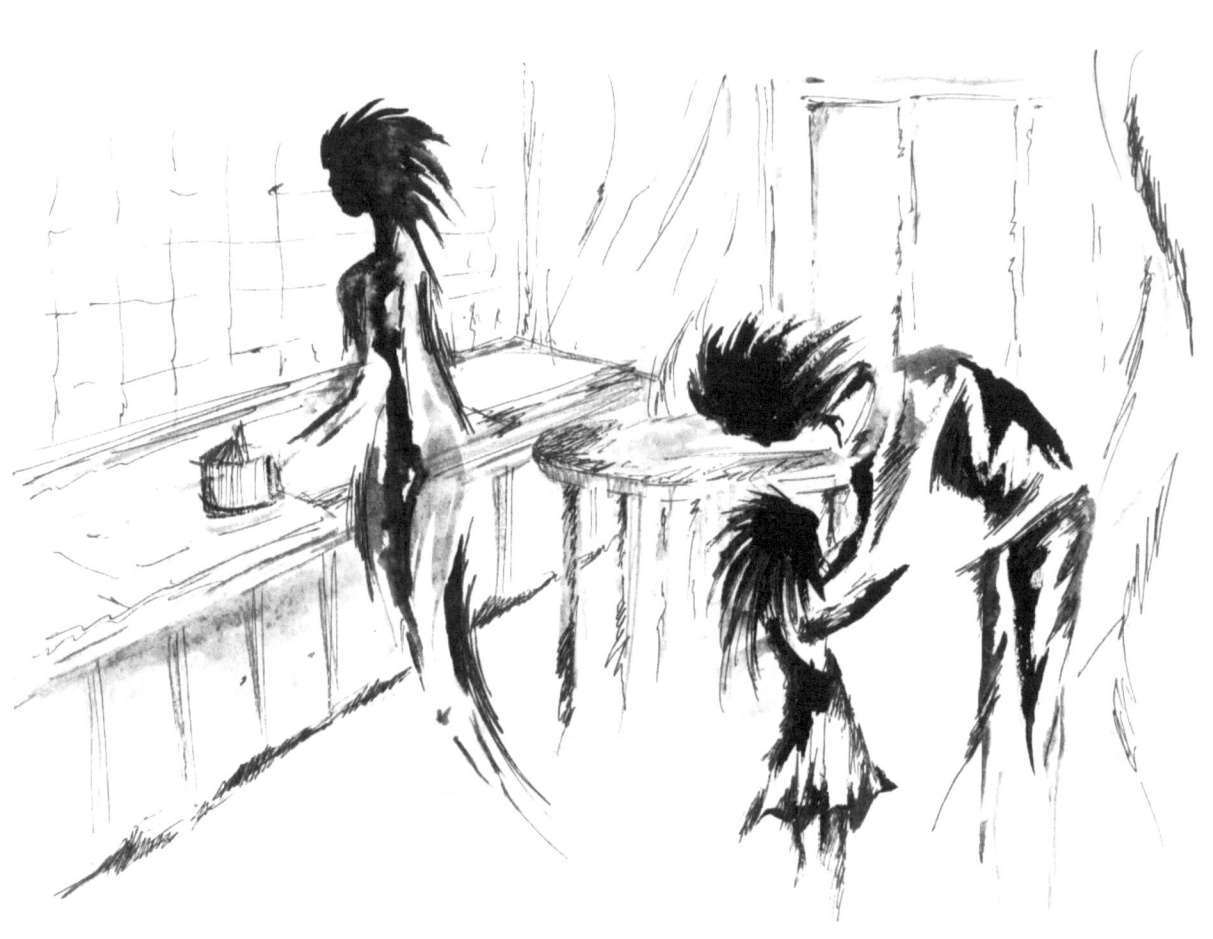

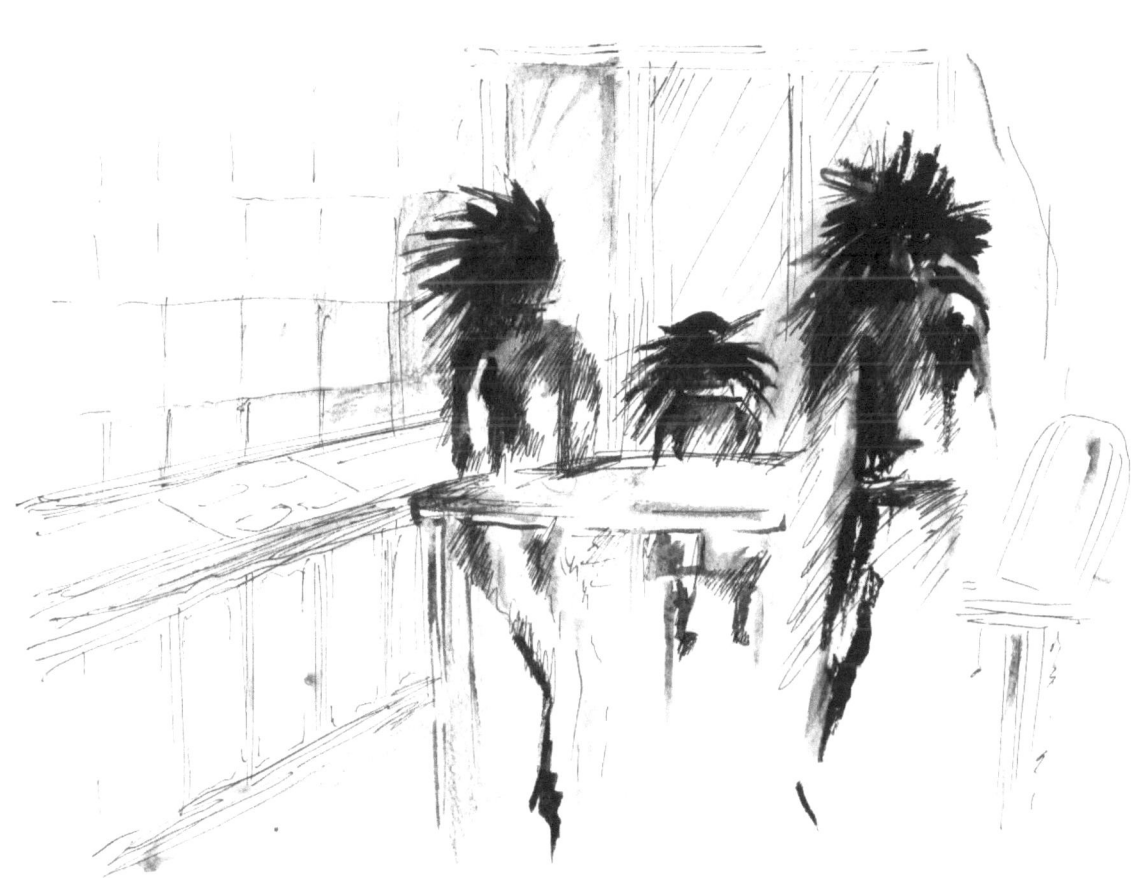

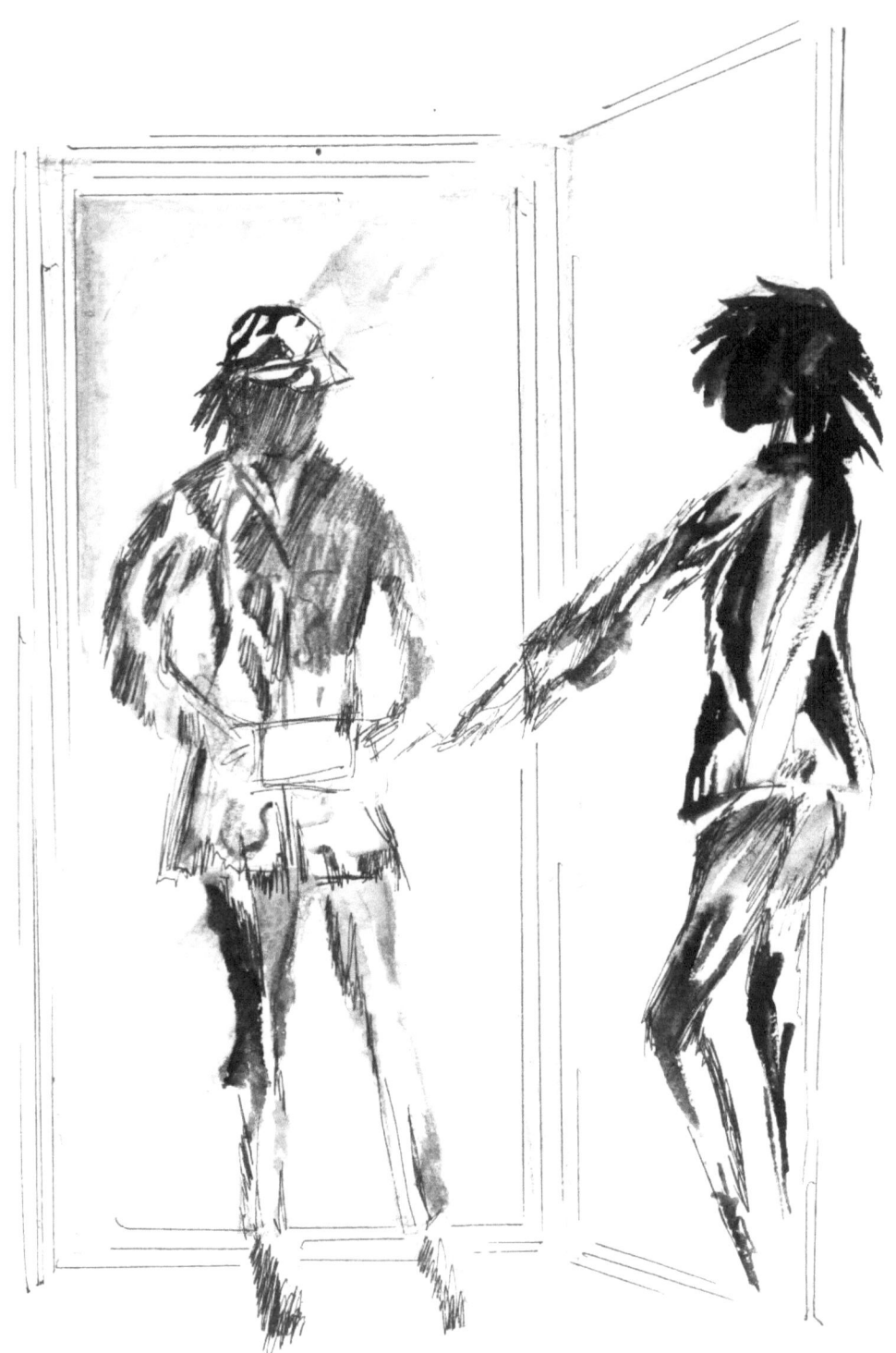

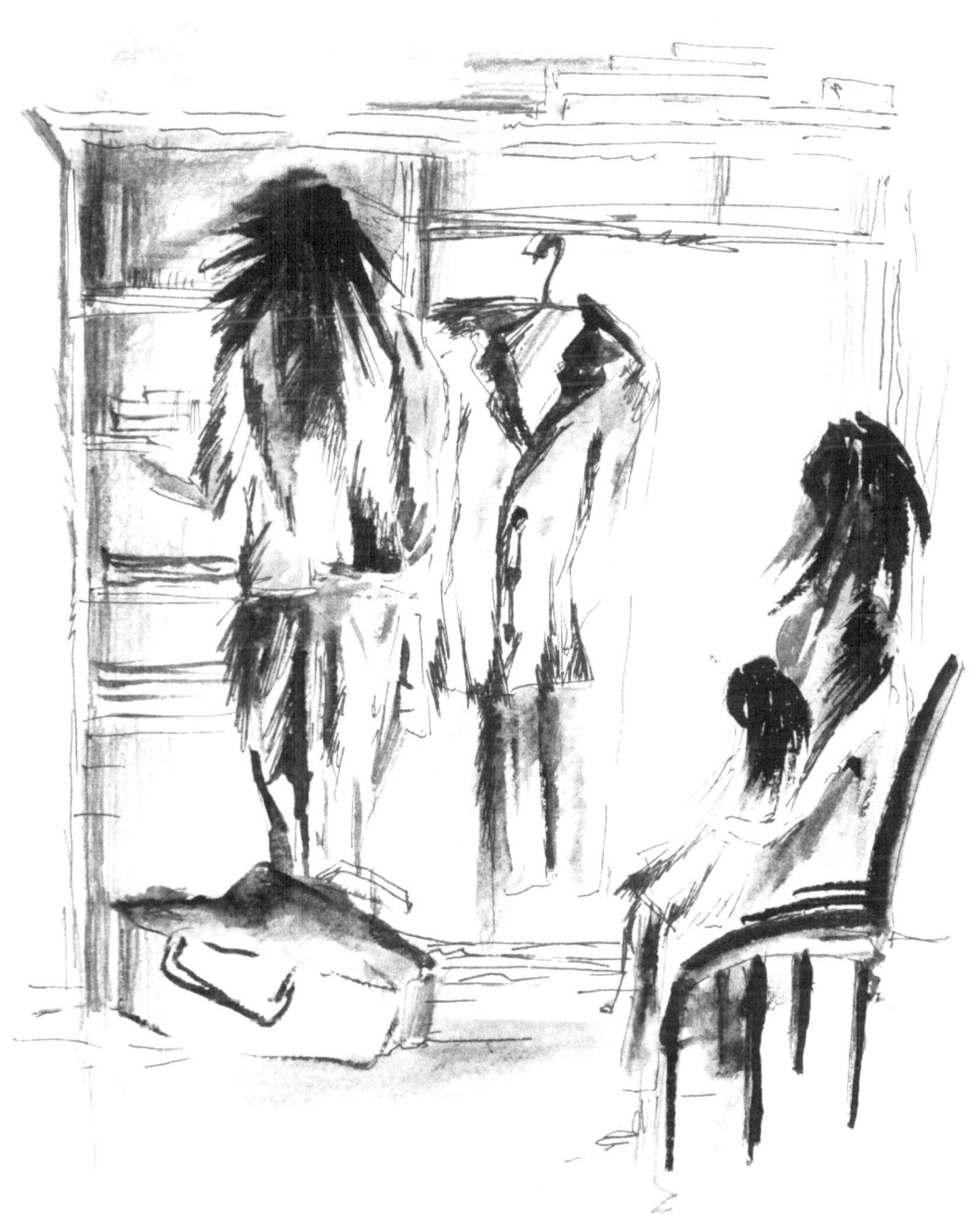

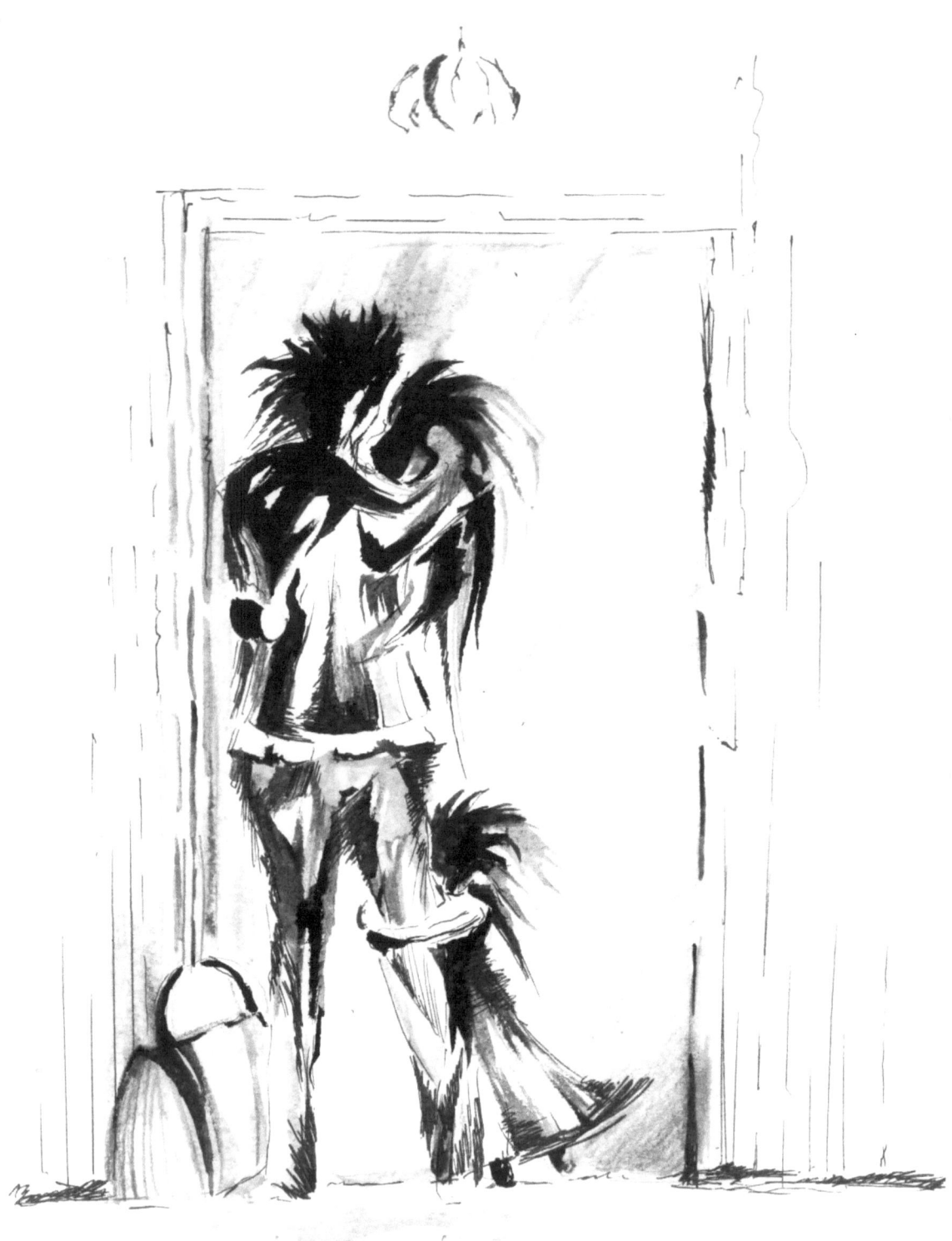

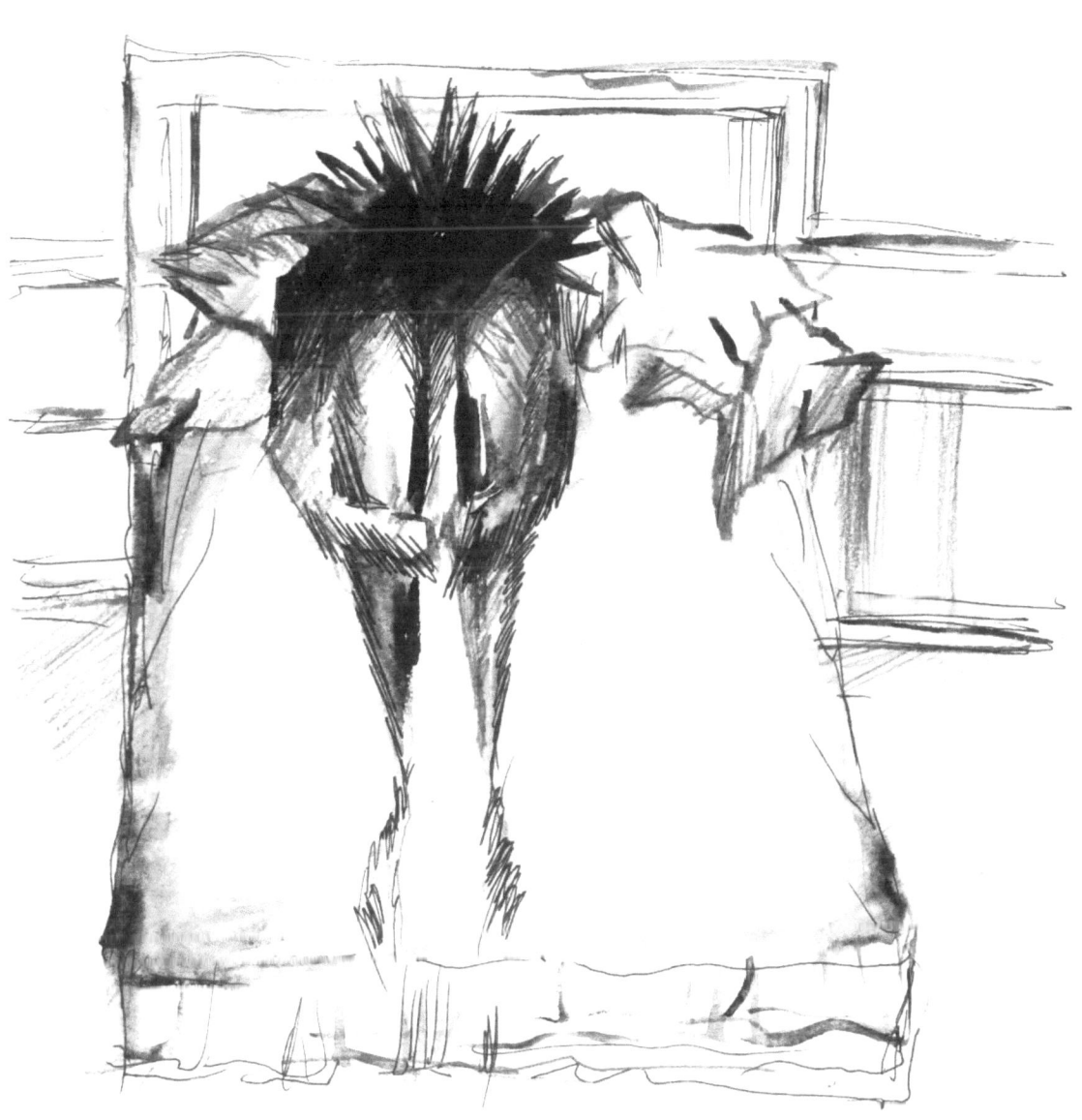

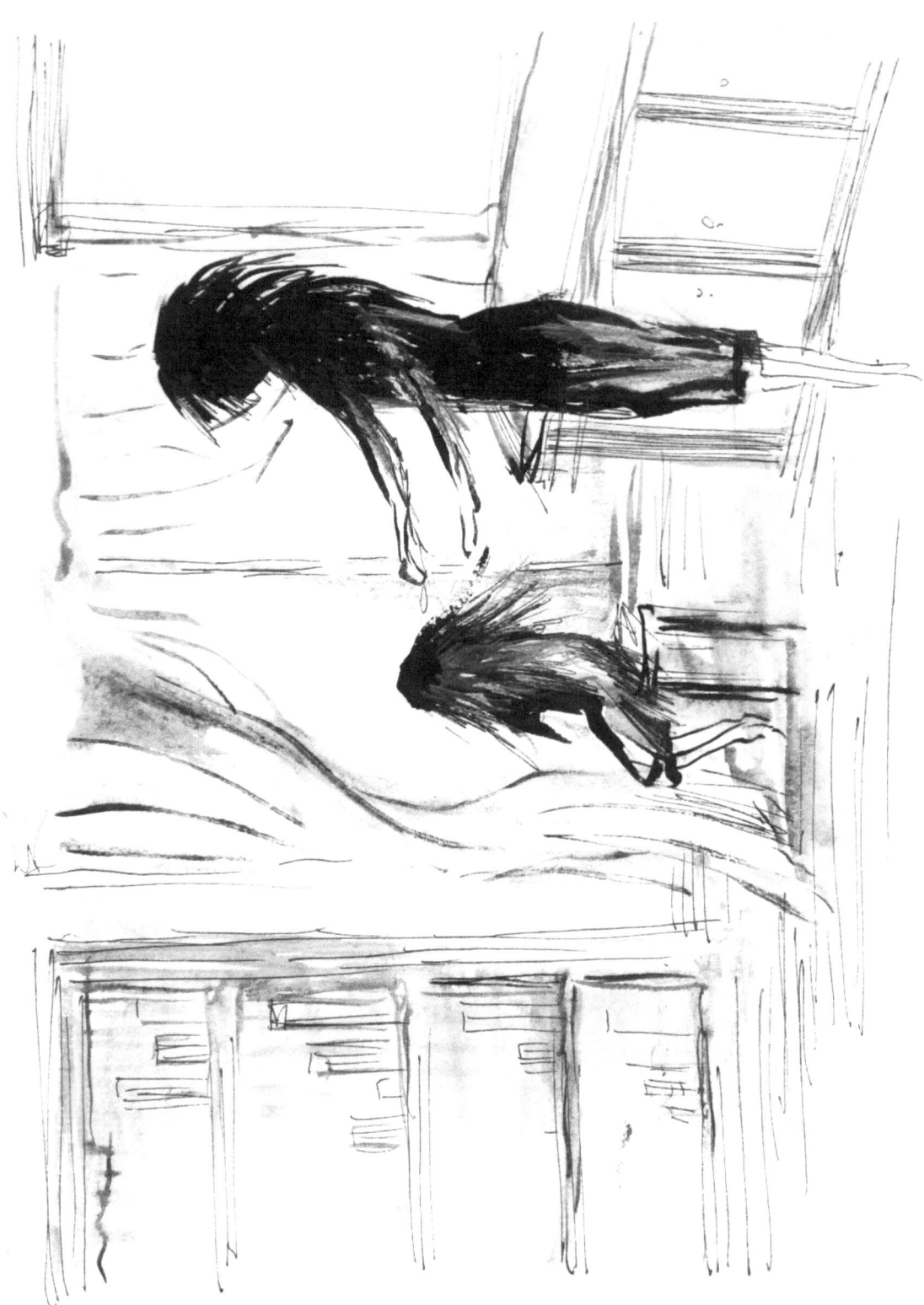

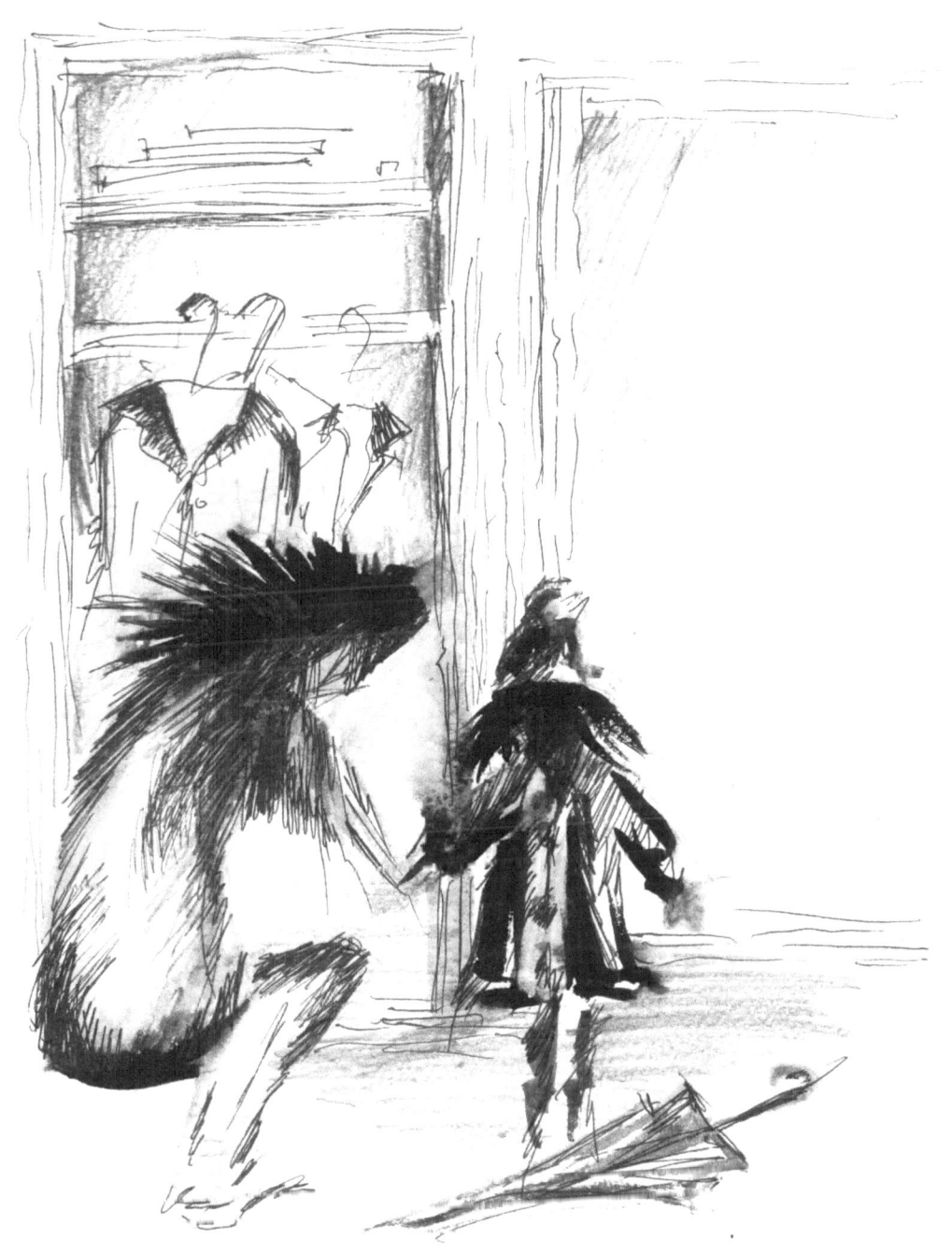

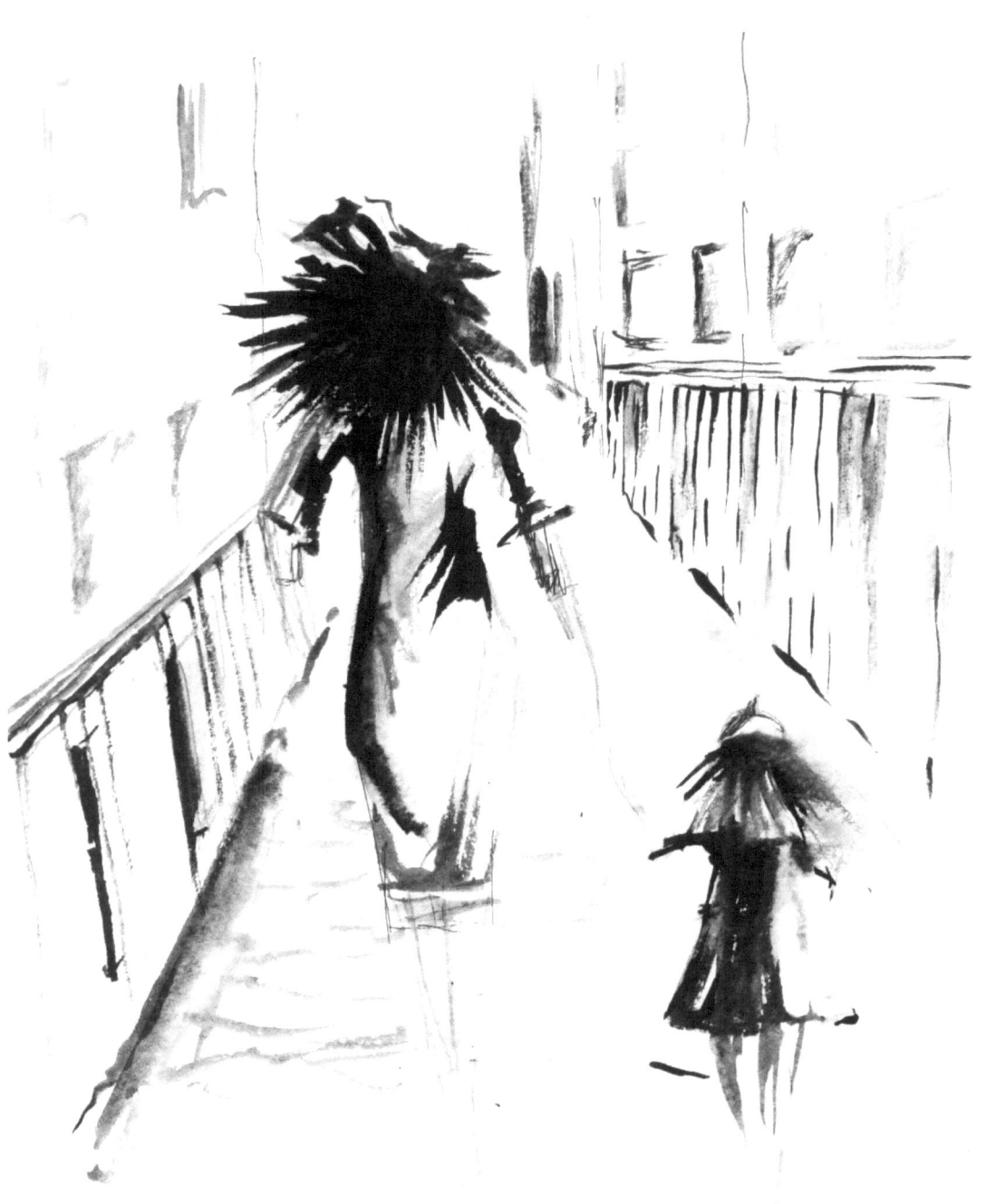

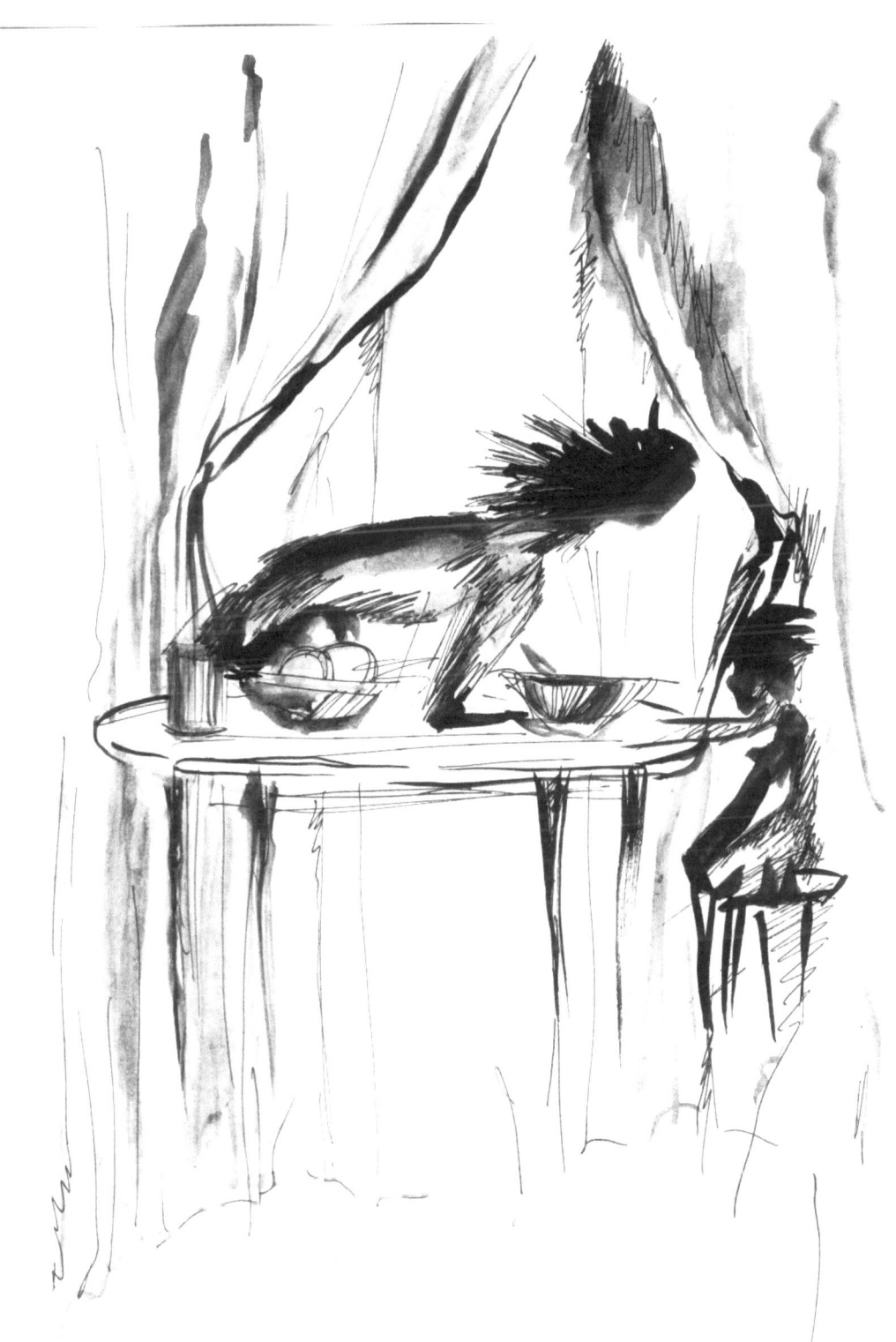

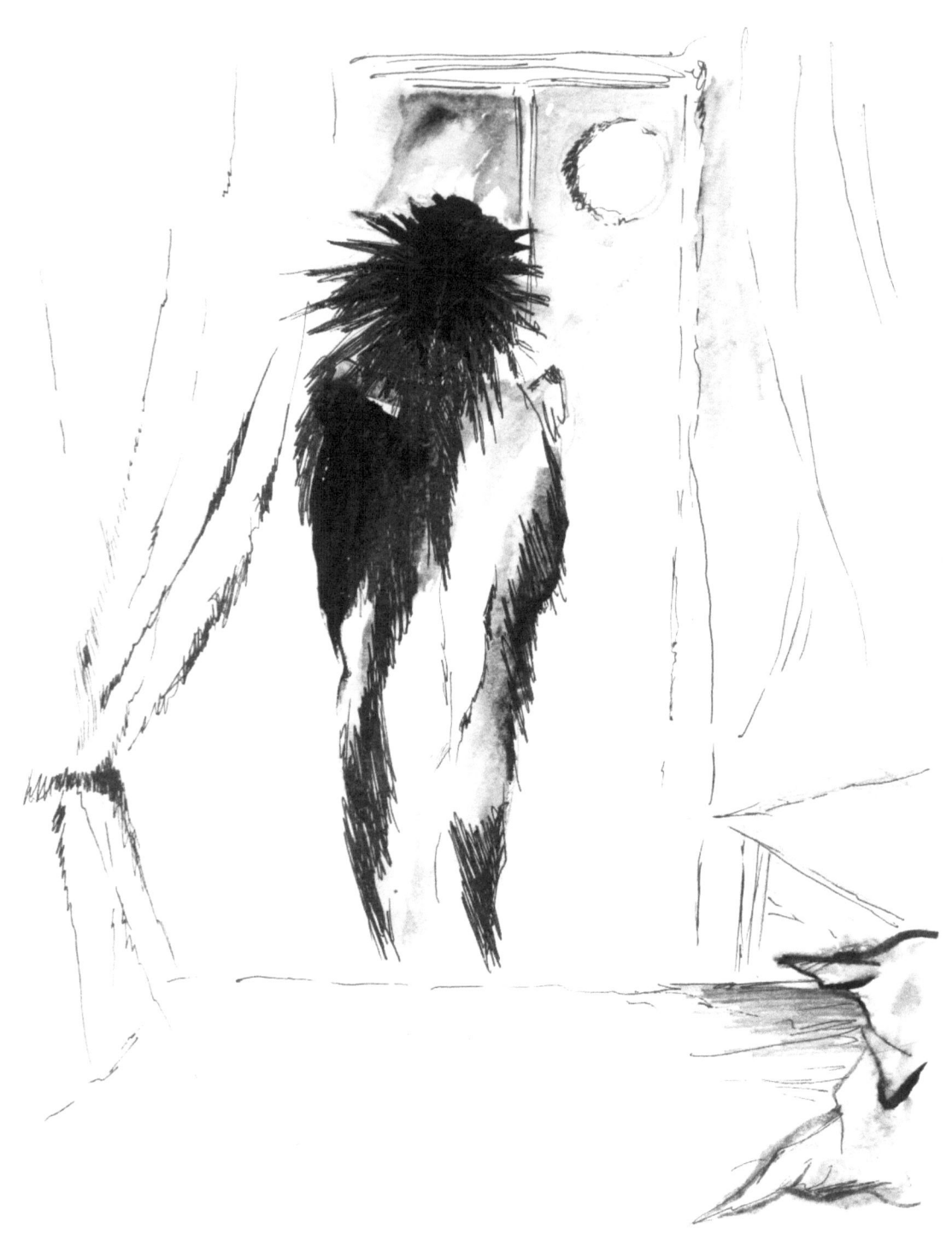

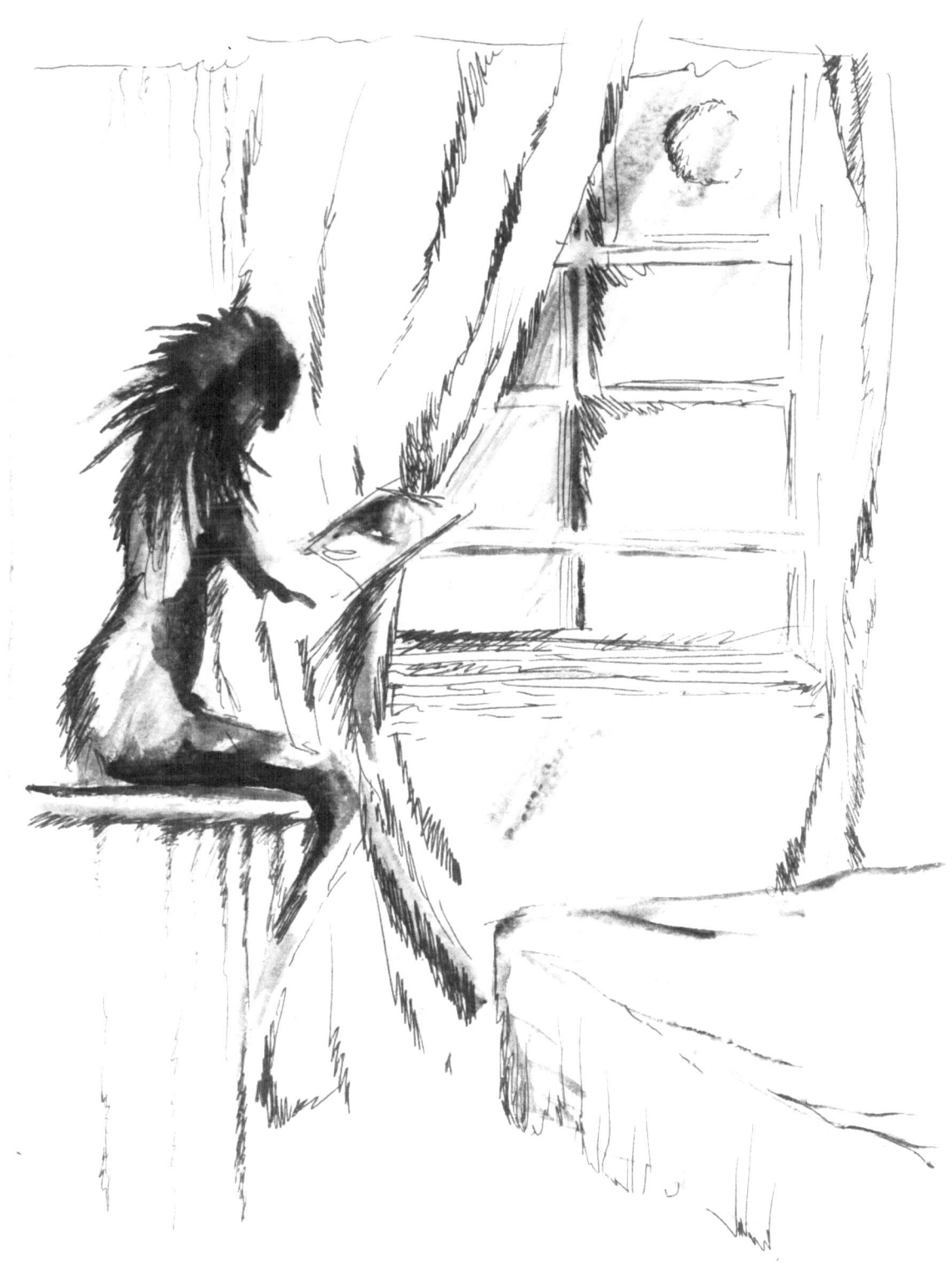

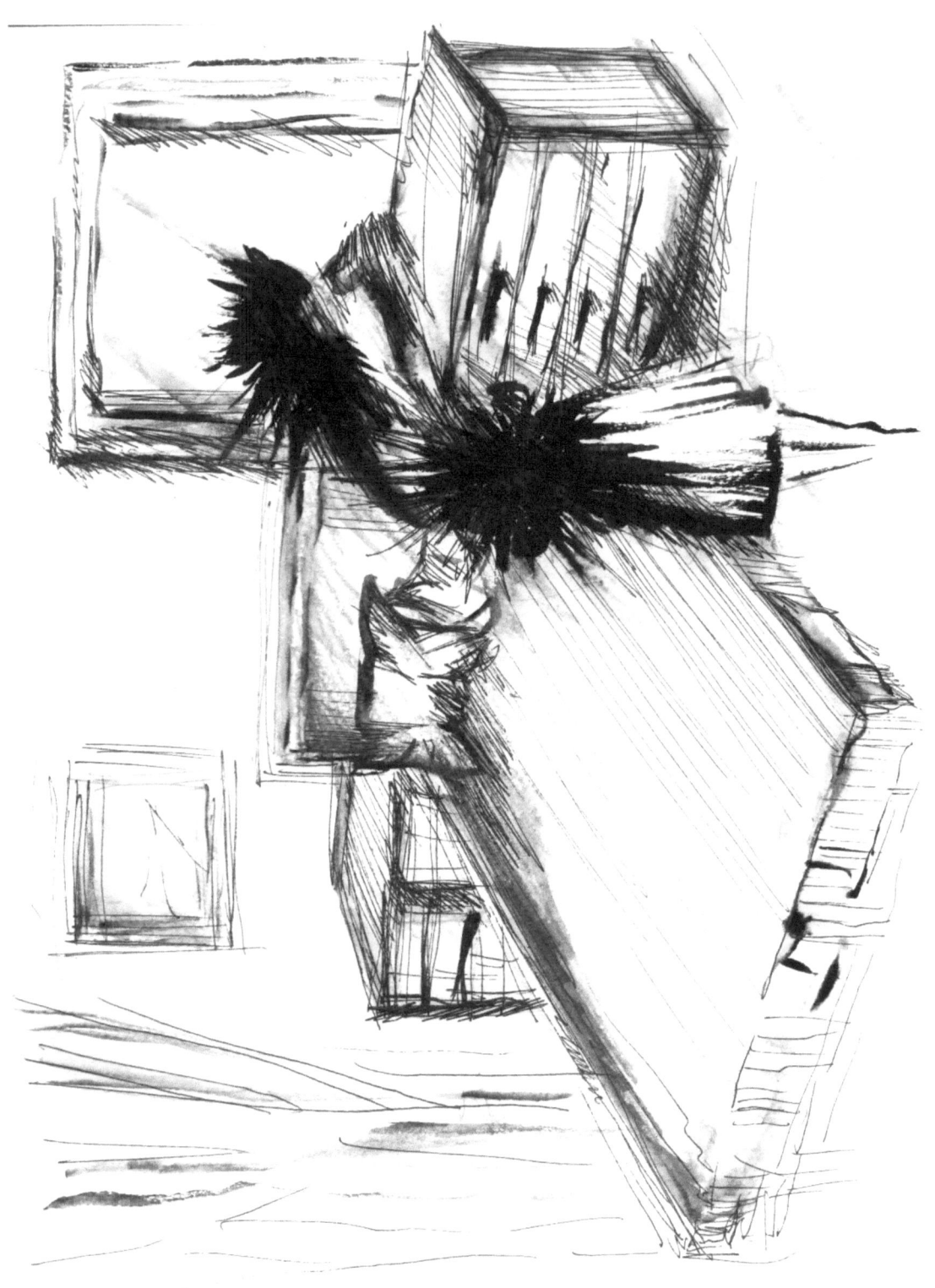

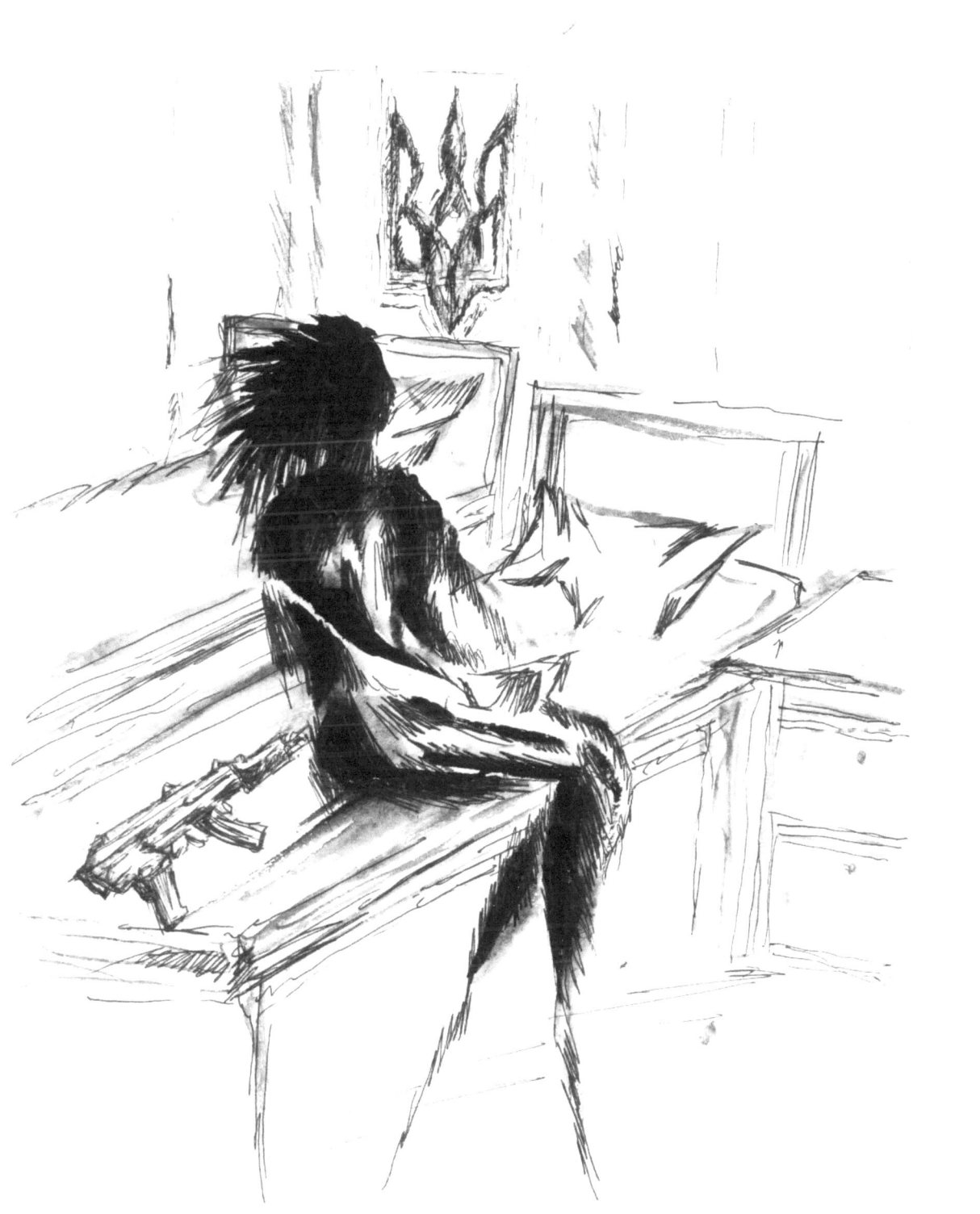

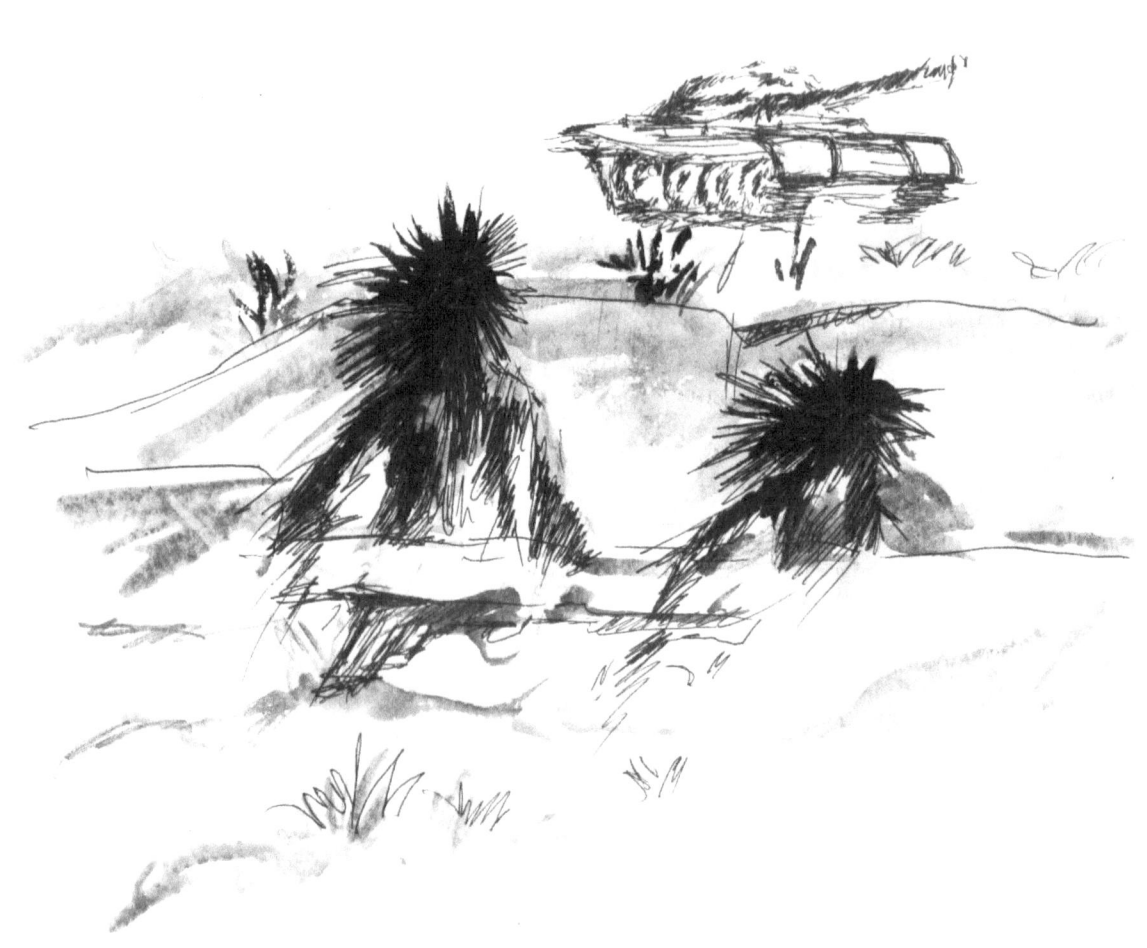

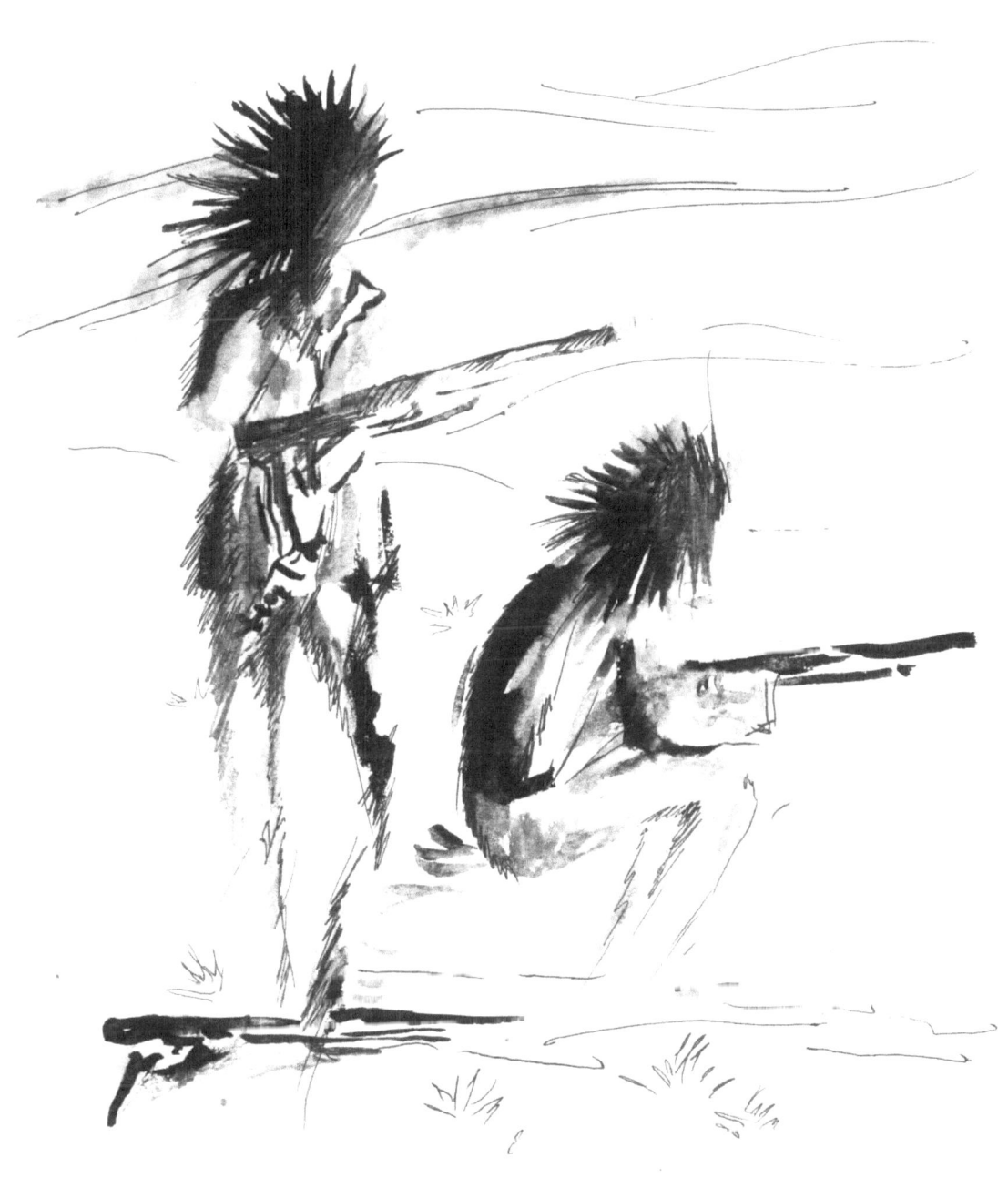

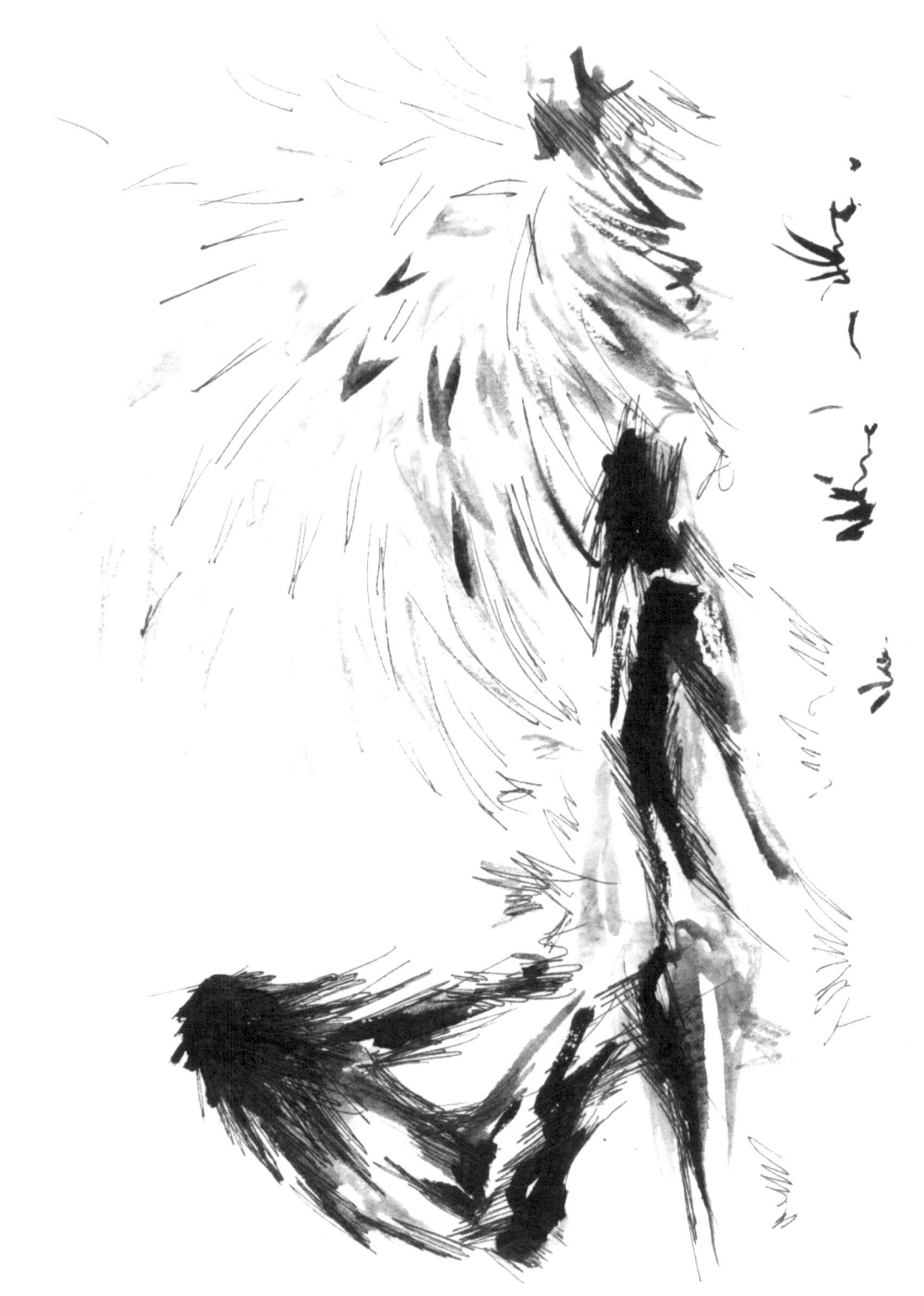

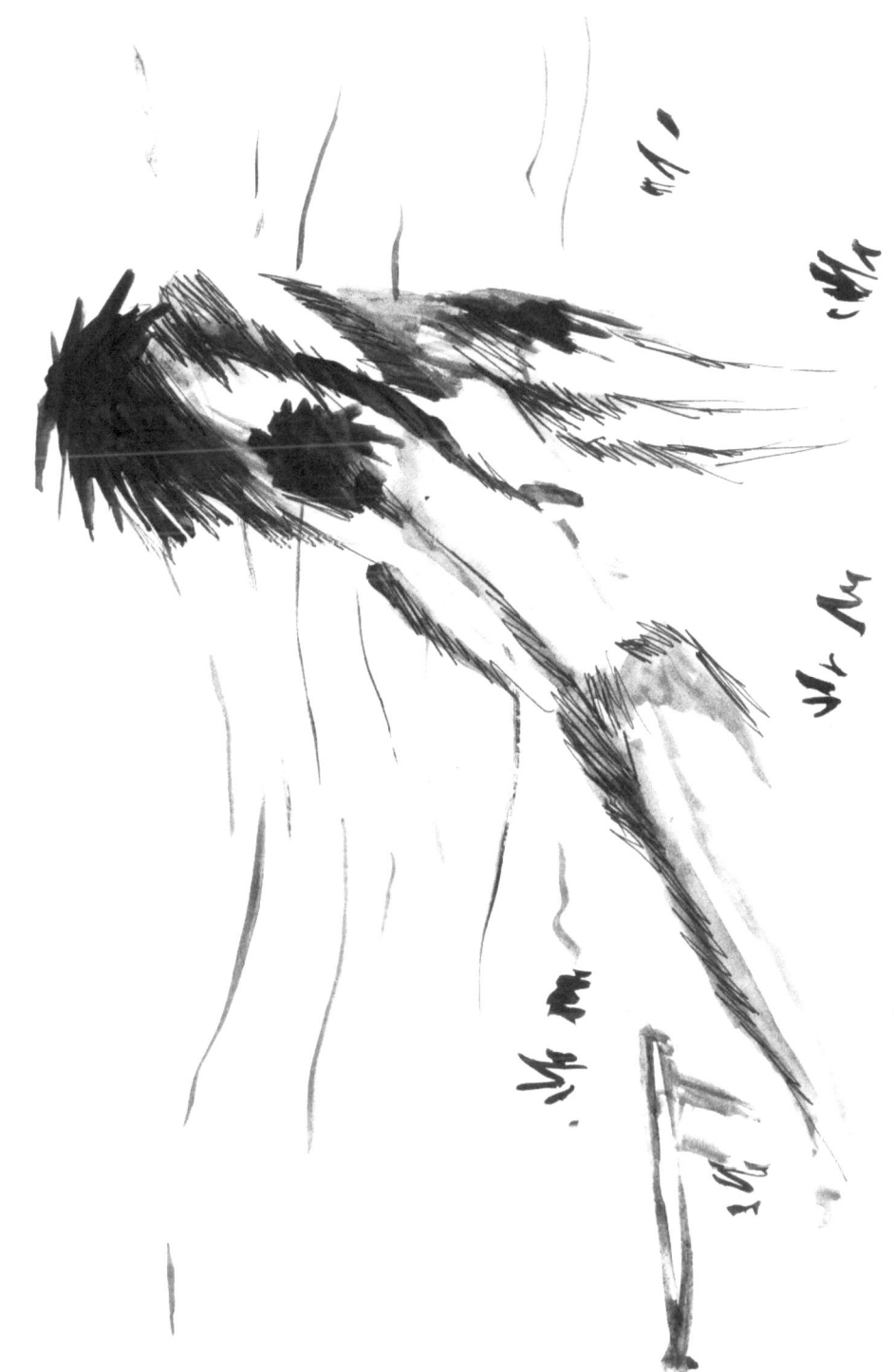

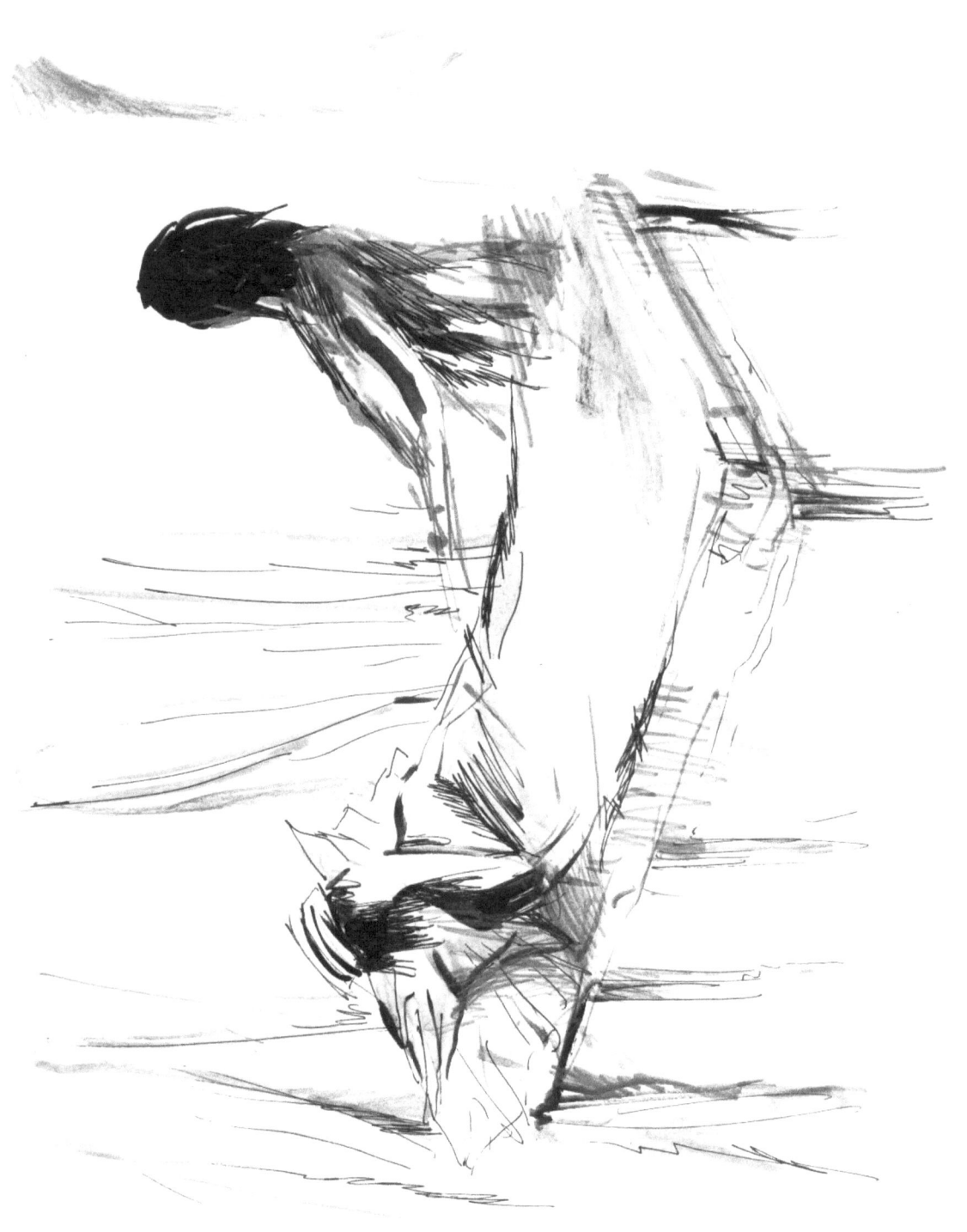

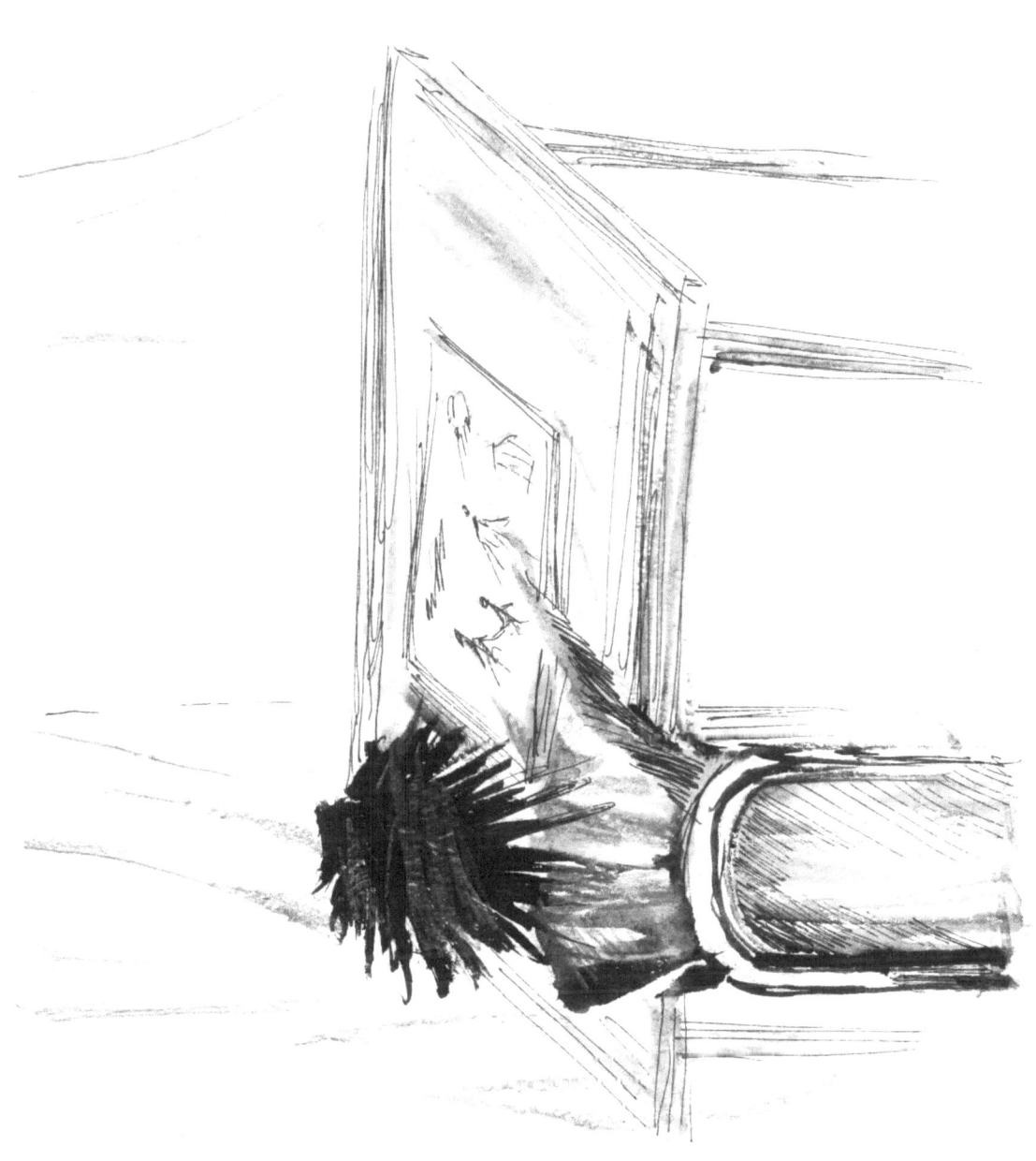

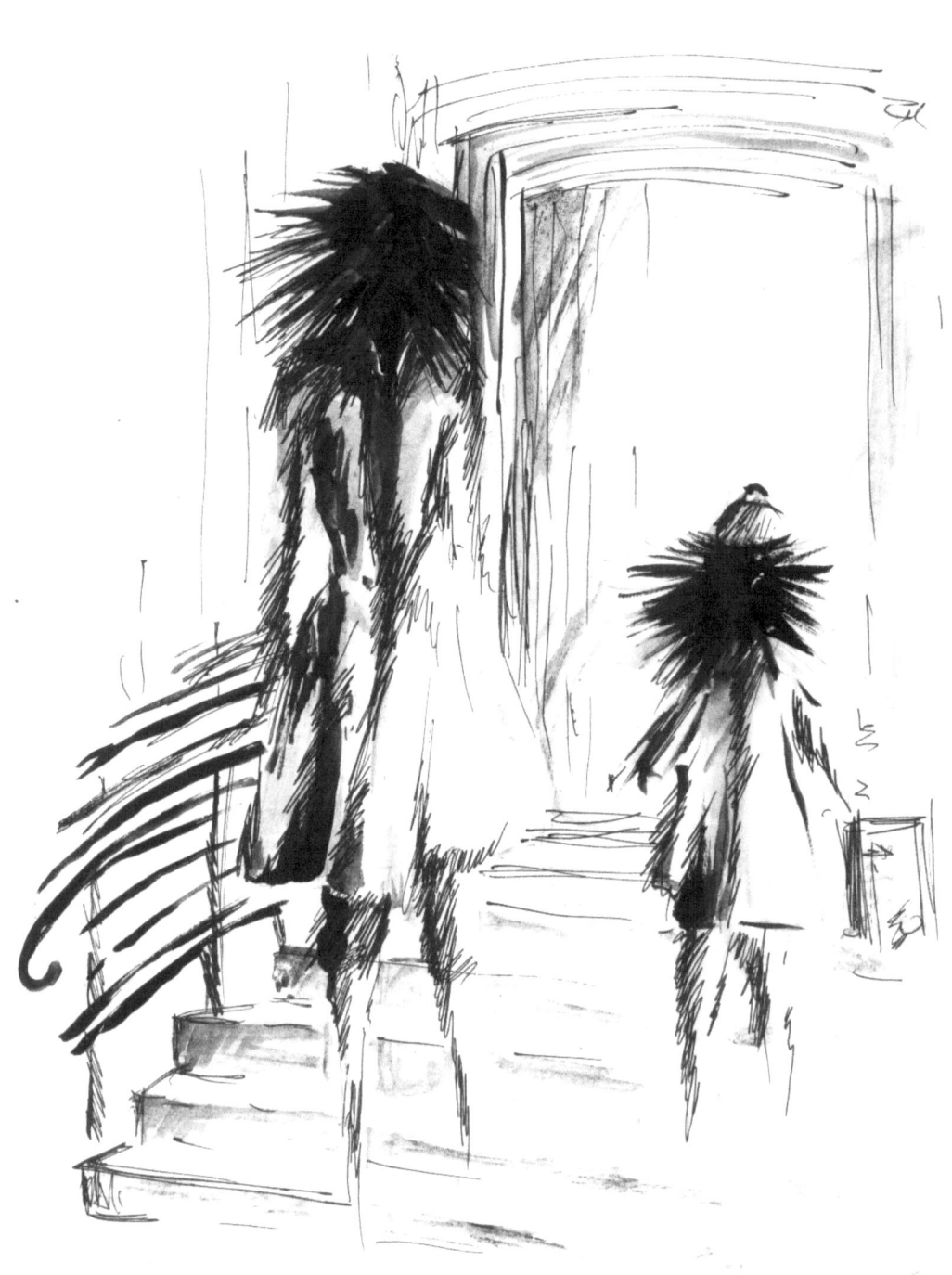

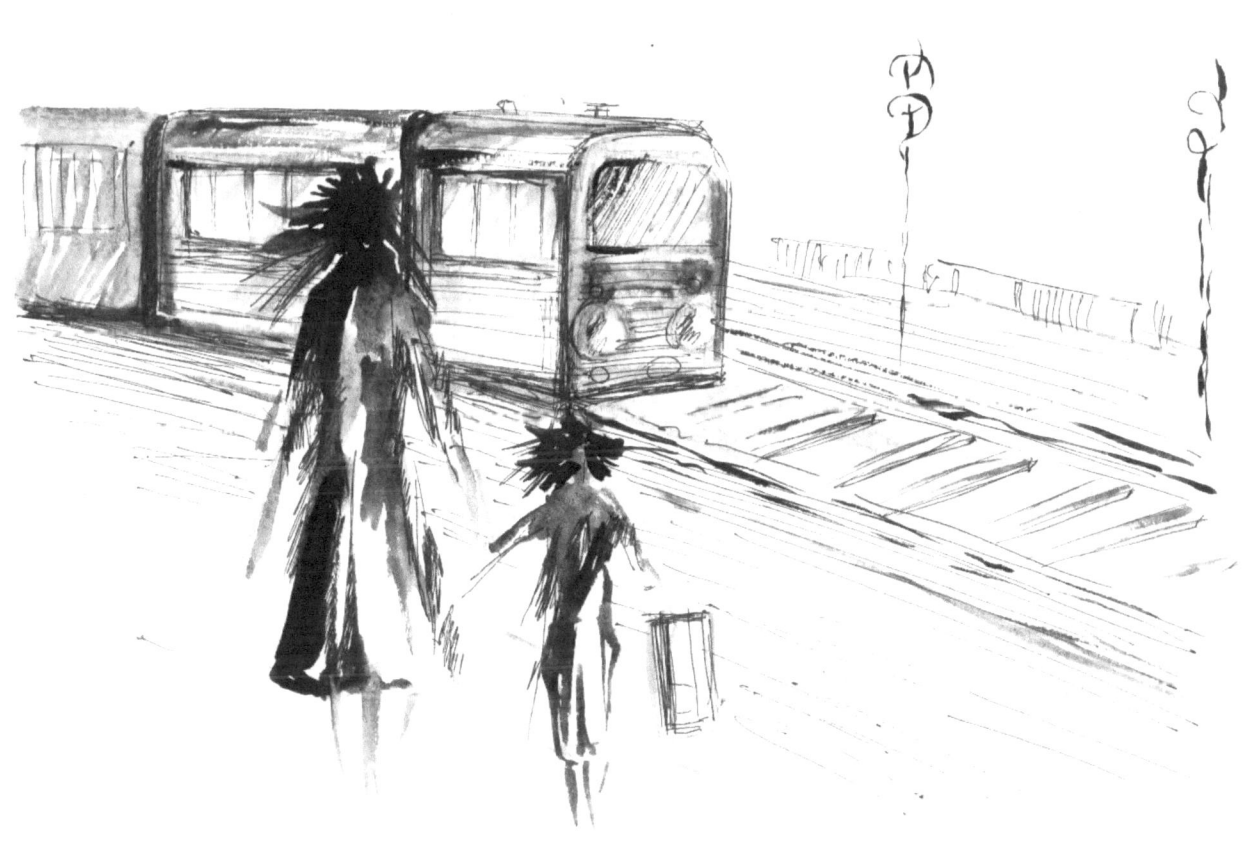

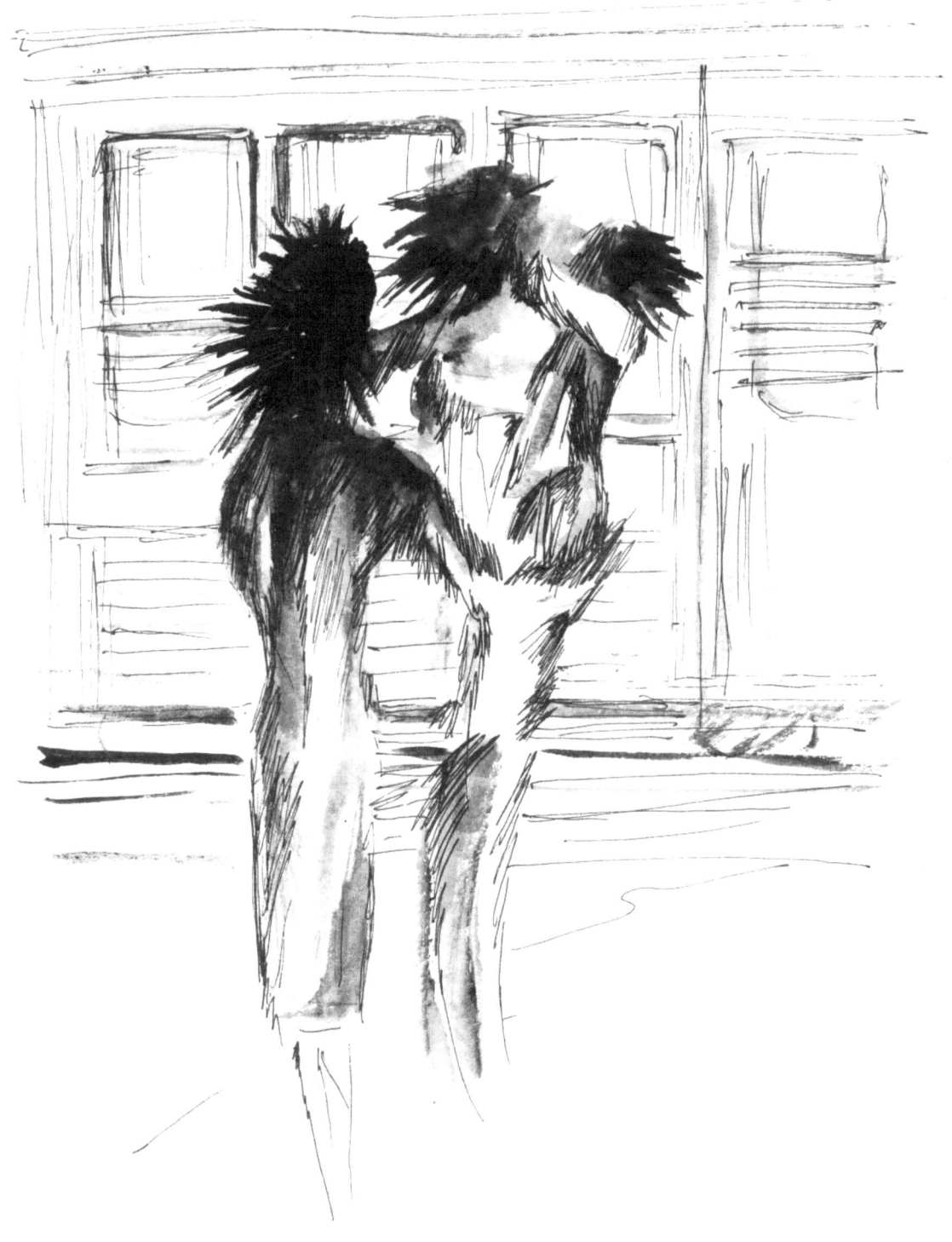